YASOLOGY VOL. I

Yasology
Vol. I

YASMIN Y. GLINTON

Yasology Vol. I

Copyright © 2021 by Yasmin Y. Glinton
Published by 45 Drafts Press
Nassau, The Bahamas

All rights reserved. No part of this publication may be reproduced, stored in a retrieval system, or transmitted, in any form or in any means—by electronic, mechanical, photocopying, recording or otherwise—without prior written permission from the author.

First Printing: 2021

Cover Design By: Sam_designs1 @fiverr

ISBN: 978-0-578-99115-3

For Me

You don't
have to look
beyond yourself
to find someone
worthwhile

You are needed

your laughter
your love

even your sorrow
softens the hearts
of others

We have been trained to believe
a job will define who we are.

A job can never define the
depth of our heart and soul.

>	No job
>	Nor title
>	can inspire
>	others.

It is you.

You inspire

You bring hope

You are who
people search for.

There is no ideal woman or man.

We are all living unique lives with circumstances and situations, hearts and emotions that are drastically different from others.

How someone acts and responds does not make them more of a man or woman than you or me.

You can only be who you are.

Who you are takes you through life's journey with a sense of peace and dignity.

Let that person grow and develop.

Be that person every day with all your might.

If you are into comparing, then you will think some days are better than others.

You will think you were better or worse at making choices.

That there were wrong decisions. Wrong moments.

You will always compare your then and now.

When we learn to stop
comparing oursleves,
we become liberators
of our mental, emotional,
and spiritual prison.

We embrace freedom.

We are mirrors of
nature.

A collection cycles
for every season.

There is no
spring without winter,
nor summer without fall

Each cycle
is important.

Each season reveals
new ways to
live our life.

Remind
yourself
you are
where you
choose to be.

When you are ready
you will choose
to be elsewhere.

**THE POWER
TO CHOOSE
IS ALWAYS
YOURS.**

There is something in this day that was meant just for you. It may be simple like a promotion or it may be grand like being told you are loved.

Know the love and light you share is ready and waiting to find its way back to you.

Do not hold grudges when someone leaves.

They are making room for others: ones you need and ones who need you.

You are not alone.

You never have been.

Allow the people moving
in and out of your
life sustain you.

Many times, we're looking for someone to say they're sorry. But we begrudge giving those sincere words to others. If you are like me, you almost never give them to yourself.

Many times, we are hurt by others. Most of the time we hurt ourselves. and bury the hurt instead of acknowledging we need to forgive ourselves.

I hope we learn to confront the hurt in us. I hope we practice forgiveness that it is more than words.

I hope we truly forgive the source of our sorrow: others and ourselves.

It is hard to face the troubles and the inadequacies we see in the world and in ourselves.

Thank you for getting up.

Thank you for daring to hope and dream and love in this world.

Thank you for sharing yourself even when you think you are not enough.

> Know you have always been enough.

You have something to say that is worth hearing. Do not lose your voice out of fear or social expectation. Never let yourself drown in your own screams.

You were given your own experiences with a mind and a heart unique to you. What you have to say is valuable.

It is important.

Your delivery is
as important as
what needs to be said.

Merge the two.
Find the balance.
Let your voice be heard.

One moment could never account for twenty-four hours.

Don't allow an incident, that took less than ten minutes to occur, be the factor that decides how you spend the rest of your day.

The true is same with life. Do not allow the hurt of a month or a year define how you interact with others and with yourself.

Life is a growing process.
Don't get stuck!
Keep growing.

Allow painful moment to pass.
Learn what you can and remain true
to yourself not the person that is
hurt or the one causing the hurt.

You are shaped and moulded from dirt into a walking, talking, logical and emotional being.

And, there are people that take comfort in your presence and love being with you.

Every year emerges a new you who hopes, dreams and accomplishes, which gives others hope that anything is possible.

If you ever need to be reminded of something beautiful, of a blessing that never ends and of hope; you only need to look at yourself.

You are an endless possibility.

When you feel overwhelmed
take a minute.

Let all the impossible and
negative things fall away.

They are fleeting.

Your ability to give hope and
love is always constant.

You are the manifestation of dreams, hope and love.

You walk these beautiful gifts into people's lives.

You have never been an option to someone. You have always been the reason for joy, be it a moment or years.

You are cared for. You and all your quirks are loved, appreciated and valued.

Nothing about today will be the same as any day you've encountered.

Every day you are given the opportunity to do something new, to define who you are.

A new day is filled with so many possibilities. But we often get caught up in the familiar process that we think every smile, laugh, growl of frustration, disappointment, and joy is just like the next.

> It isn't.

Today,
you can choose
to be the person
you envision, or
you can go with
the usual flow.

The choice will always be yours.

We are all a source of light and inspiration.

We were created with the sole purpose of illuminating this world with the uniqueness of our being.

We are so extraordinary that each strand of our hair was made individually.

There is a power in us that cannot be contained nor explained. Our light has the ability to exceed our life.

That is the kind of power that exists in us.

We have to be
in the business:
of seeing people
      and acknowledging
their presence as worthwhile.

We should not get so caught up
in selection and preference that
we dehumanize or belittle the
importance of another human.

When we see beyond the idea of liking or disliking and we love the human race as a whole, then we can become a people that have accomplished something.

Forgiveness, courage, compassion and love should be our most frequent currency.

Learning to operate them on a daily basis should be our goal.

We need it for ourselves and for others.

Dreams are beautiful beginnings. They are a projection of things to come.

But dreams require hours at the drawing board. They demand resilience and the determination to try again.

Dreams require consistency,
hard work and faith.

They require you
believing in them.

Taking moments to appreciate who we are and what we have is important.

It is easy to get caught up preparing for the next thing on our list.

We have been wired to believe setting and obtaining goals are our purpose.

It is not.

Sometimes we need to be in awe of what we have we have accomplished and who we have become.

Don't forget we were once a being that could not talk or walk.

Look at who we are now and the odds we have overcome.

When we are dissatisfied, it is never because of where we are.

It is always because of what we believe about where we are.

Everything we have
or need stems from
what we
believe you
deserve.

There are many ways to look at life. We decide each day what we think about ourselves.

We must choose wisely.

Our spiritual, emotional and mental stability stem from it.

Do not regret the lessons
after you've already enjoyed
making the choice.

Lessons always follow the
choices we make.

You will never have one
without the other.

Sometimes, we have to allow ourself to see things from every angle.

It is easy to be trapped in our thinking for months or years and that can be unhealthy.

Remember things are never what they seem.

We will never get the full picture when we're in the middle of our growth.

Don't hold onto an image of yourself that doesn't show the potential of your growth from every angle.

Don't hold onto the worst of someone else.

Sometimes
what we do best
is allow others
the freedom to
be themselves.

Beyond what a person does or
the role they play in our lives
we remember most the moments
we felt free to be ourselves in
their company.

May we make it a point to
allow the individuals in our
life that same freedom.

Life is rough.

Sometimes you get picked up and kicked about in the same spot that was already sore and abused.

It is not always easy for someone to reach out.

It does not mean they do not care.

Sometimes, life is simply hard, and we have to learn to live through their absence, without judgement.

For those to weary to reach out
know you are loved.

If you can reach out then do so,
remind someone they are loved.

Sometimes the hardest thing for us to do is try.

Trying is the only way to rid ourselves of the fear and the uncertainty.

It is the only way we figure out the answer to what could I be.

Let your actions define you not fear or doubt.

**Try it.
Say it.
Do it.**

Give yourself some credit. There are more good things happening for you than you think.

Try to live through the day thinking only positive things, not only about others but also yourself.

We often rehash what we have done wrong, which may be five or six events in our life that overpower the 20-30-50 things we had done right.

It seems a bit ludicrous to relive the worst when there is opportunity to ground yourself in the multitude of things you have done right.

Decide to try again tomorrow.

Bask in knowing you had the courage to go through another day despite the obstacles that were in front of you.

You went to bed knowing what you would face, but you decided tomorrow will not be the same as yesterday.

You were determined not to be overwhelmed by circumstances.

If no one else says it:
I am grateful for that choice.
I am grateful you are still here.

We reflect something holy and divine.

Scientist tell us we get oxygen from trees, but everyone once and a while I remind myself that we keep the trees alive.

We are responsible for the fact that other creatures live.

Sometimes we are responsible for creating another life.

Sometimes we are the reason someone gets up and tries.
The reason others love.

We-- you and I are that important.

If we want to grow beyond the place, we are at, we have to eventually let go.

We all know the things that hold us to a place: fears, expectations, hope for change.

Sometimes we spend so long existing in this blank space that we lose ourselves in them.

**WE LET GO TO
LEARN SOMETHING
WE NEVER KNEW.**

**WE TRY TO
MAKE ROOM FOR
NEW OPPORTUNITIES.**

Do not be so enamoured with the idea of how you want to live that you fail to allow the wonders of living to occur.

The reality is you can plan to be at a location, but that plan will never determine what happens when you get there.

The only thing we can really plan is showing up.

Sometimes you need a vacation from all the expectations you and others have placed on yourself.

There must be a specific time set aside for you to be free, to relax, to unwind. There must be time planned for you to let your restrictions, requirements and deadlines go.

These moments should be strategically planned because they keep us grounded.

It does not have to be extravagant; it just has to feed peace into your soul.

You are a testament of love. That is why you never realize when you begin loving. It is because you are love.

You are love on your good days. You are love on your bad days. You are love when you are lonely and longing for it.

When
you're
searching
for love
seek
yourself.

Every day you have an opportunity to explore the world any way you desire.

It is never too late.
As long as there is breath,
there is an opportunity.

You are the risk you won't regret it.

We often forget that people change just as we do.

Sometimes we hold onto a grudge or a love that stirred deep emotions in us. And, we stay in that moment.

We don't allow ourselves to see the development of that person beyond that moment. We are controlled more by that moment than any other rational or logic.

Sometimes the best thing to do is lay those memories to rest.

Everything we have ever needed or desired to be is already in us.

Most of the time we wait for circumstance to reveal it.

Manifestation arrives
when we are ready to
release it.

Take this moment to say-- I am capable.

Know that it is true. You are capable:

> of leaving
> of staying
> of trying
> of being more.
> of dreaming
> of letting go
> of loving.

You are able to do anything you set your mind to.

You are able of doing the very thing(s) that set your soul free.

In our society, it's easy to add our comment, or click like to show our agreement.

We've become talkers with no drive to do.

But at the end of the day, it is the doing that we must pursue.

It is only when we do we see change and development in life, in relationships with others, in our country and the world.

TALKING CHANGE IS GOOD.

BEING CHANGE IS IMPERATIVE.

We must never succumb to the belief that we are alone.

When on our individual journey to discover who we are, we impact and are impacted by others.

What we do, who we become is important to all.

We are not alone.

The world is all here with you.

And it is grateful for our life.

You have always been a beauty to behold.

You have always been a possibility.

You have always been the real deal.

You are so many things no one can truly define you.

That's what makes you extraordinary. You evolve and sometimes you don't even know it. And sometimes you do and it's painful. But you do it over and over again anyway.

You are the very essence of possibilities.

Be yourself.

And, if you have no idea who that is then take the time to figure you out.

Be yourself unapologetically. This person is bursting with ideas, affection and love destined to touch specific lives.

There are lives only you can touch.

So, forget what you think you should look like, be who you desire most.

That person is needed.

The world needs you.

It needs you in your most comfortable form.

It needs you in the skin you're confident in.

It needs you in the truth of who you are.

Being wrong is an opportunity for you to learn to be more aware, determined, focused, kinder- wiser.

It is a moment of growth.

It is a moment where you expand your horizon. You receive tools to see someone or a situation in a way you never have before.

Failure is an opportunity to try again.

Lots of times we find ourselves in negative situations.

The trouble with being in these situations is that we become cruel, harsh, and despondant.

We forget we have a choice.

We either allow the situation to determine how we react, or we determine how we act in the situation.

Emotional maturity begins with understanding we control how we think and how we act no matter the situation.

Forgiveness is hard work.

It takes
effort and
requires
loyalty.

Forgiveness is a full-time job.

Free yourself by being who you have always desired.

May we always show
up with patience and
a willing heart.

May we show up with
the love we wish others
to extend to us when we
need to be forgiven.

We often judge if we are good people by the way we treat loved ones.

But, our character is tested by strangers and how we treat those we would not want to spend more than ten minutes with.

Do we scorn them and wear a face of disgust? Do we smile in their face and tear them apart behind their back?

We show our character by what we say about these people when we're comfortable and when they aren't in hearing distance. Those moments define who we truly are.

Remember even those we don't see eye to eye with also need to be treated with respect in our thoughts and in our deeds.

Life never waits until we are ready.

Things happen if we planned them or not. They don't consult if we are ready for them or not.

There is not really a place of readiness, there is only faith and courage. Without these, we may spend our whole lives waiting on right moments.

Every day you live is
the right moment.

It is the only moment you have.

You are it!

Whatever you have been looking or waiting for is you.

We haven't been taught to value getting to know who we are, and as a result as we get older, we seem to 'finally' find ourselves.

Take the risk now. Find out who you are beyond the job, the relationship and family expectations.

Listen and trust that the person you find is just who you were looking for. Just who you were waiting for.

You are unique.

In all of earth's history
the one thing that has
never existed is you.

Who you are and the choices you
make change the world.

You and every person that exists in
your world are the difference.

Live scary dreams
Love for loving sake
Speak the truth of your
heart with a gentle voice.

History
understands
it is privileged to
bear witness to you.

The crazy thing about having plans set in stone is that we don't account for how we will change and grow when we finally reach our destination.

Sometimes after intense dreaming and planning we reach our dream, but it no longer suits us.

Instead of finding what does, we cling to that dream for years. We make our life miserable because we can't let go.

Don't hold your self-hostage to things of the past that no longer suit you.

The greatest disservice we do to the people in our life is being to busy to reach out to them.

We take it in stride that one's life becomes so busy that it's acceptable not to reach out to someone.

But the reality is, our own busyness could never compete with reassuring and affirming someone of our love of them.

Doing 'stuff' should never be the reason you have not called, visited, or even just sent a text to say hi.

If we are caught in our doing, then how can we request time from others and be hurt when it is not given?

Remember how you treat others will eventually find its way back to you.

Life has to take its course.

No matter how fast you want things to happen.

No matter how much you think you are ready.

Sometimes our journey is held up because we have to meet certain people, people who change the way we see the life we have and how we walk.

These people give us strength and courage. Some break us down so that we can rebuild with a clearer vision than what we had before. And we need them to offer us room to redefine ourselves as we journey.

So, do not worry if you are not storming through life. There is someone right where you are who is meant to change your life, or whose life you are meant to change. It will not always be sunshine, but you'll always have a reason for being right where you are.

No matter what you do or say, there will be a positive and negative reaction.

Do not act to prove anyone right or wrong.

Act because your heart demands it. Act because you cannot sleep without thinking about what you want to do. Act because the desire wakes you up in the morning.

Take action because it is a part of who you are.

Be who you are without ill intentions towards others.

Live with a love of self that rids you the fear of judgement from others.

Find it in your heart to forgive yourself.

Accept that there was a point in time when you knew no better, so you could do no better.

Then put it to rest.

And, give yourself the opportunity to make another choice.

Sometimes we have to face the reality that we allow others to mistreat us.

We allow it out of fear, for the sake of acceptance, because it's what we think is normal, or because we think it's what we deserve.

The truth is if we don't improve the way we see ourself and how we feel about who we are, we will always accept mistreatment.

Not only accept it, but also solidify to others that their treatment of us is okay.

It is better to create a life where you are valued than one of suffering: mentality, physically, emotionally, and spiritually.

Here it is.

Your opportunity to be who you've dreamed.

The moment to believe in yourself.

The moment to realize loving yourself is just as important as loving others.

Here is your moment to let go of your fears and insecurities even if it's just small moment every day.

Here is Your moment.

Do what you will with it.

It is yours. There is no wrong way to live it when you live it with your dreams before your eyes and under your feet.

When neglected everything becomes an internal battle of what have I done.

Or what haven't I done enough of?

We all know what this feels like.

We know what it is to be fragile and vulnerable.

Why do we hide it?

These are the things that other beings need to know they will survive.

They need to know they will live through it.

Take courage.

There is healing.

There is light and life and laughter.

There is still hope.

Do not be afraid to lean.

Allow someone the privilege of showing you that the world has people who are caring, kind, considerate, loyal.

Allow someone the opportunity to show you just how amazing you are and what you mean to them.

We get so locked in ourselves we do not realize people need to show us love. Instead of relationships, we build walls and block people out, we stifle not only ourselves but others.

We need to allow ourself to experience the love and pleasure that someone feels just by being in our presence. Then allow ourself to return that love and joy.

Remember even though some hurt us, others heal us.

Give yourself permission to allow others to heal what you carry with their care and love.

There are times when you have to be willing to walk away in order to sustain

your mental well-being.

It's not about giving in or throwing in the towel. Sometimes it boils down to remembering your mind, spirit and heart are important. They are essential to your keeping peace within yourself and the situations you find yourself in.

Life is unpredictable.

The only thing you can be sure of is yourself and your ability to adjust to the changes in life.

The ability to change is the gift we have been given. But we often forget that we are capable of change.

We forget we are meant to change.

Don't forget how beautiful it can be to renew yourself with change.

Make a habit of being honest and realistic with yourself and others.

Nothing damages us like lies and unrealistic expectations and projections.

Refuse to create a pretence to make others comfortable. Refuse to create someone that you are uncomfortable with to be accepted.

Give the truth to others, give yourself honesty. There is a freedom in honesty that gives peace and the gift of true companionship and love.

Faith.

It's the only fuel we run on. We have faith that we will see another day. Faith that our money will be in the bank every payday. We have faith that our car will start, that water will run when we turn the tap. Basically, we live a life of faith--in everything else but ourselves.

If we were to take one ounce of that faith and pour it into developing the person we desire, what amazing people we would be.

What a changed we would create.

HAVE FAITH IN YOU.

THE PERSON YOU SEEK TO BE DESERVES IT.

Yasmin Glinton Poitier is a Nassau native with a love for creating stories through poetry. July 2018, she completed her MA in Creative Writing and Education at Goldsmiths, University of London. She is the author of *The Year She Wrote*, *At The Shore* (Current Books), and *An Olive Branch*. In her work, Glinton focuses on place, the importance of self-evaluation and relationship dynamics. She explores how relationships are defined by social expectations when we fail to question and define them ourselves. She has performed spoken word poetry in Canada and The Bahamas. Her works have appeared in Bahama Mama 2011, Gumelemi 2015, NE8, The Year She Wrote, Pattern Exhibition @ Bahamar, NE9 and Cultural and Pedagogical Inquiry Journal (CPI). Currently, Glinton is a teacher of English Language and Literature at C.V. Bethel High School, a workshop facilitator, actress, and a spoken word artist.

Instagram: @yasi.glint

Made in United States
North Haven, CT
21 March 2023